10

W9-AWO-856

# BASKETBALL

## A TRUE BOOK®

### by
### Mike Kennedy

### Children's Press®
### A Division of Scholastic Inc.

New York  Toronto  London  Auckland  Sydney
Mexico City  New Delhi  Hong Kong
Danbury, Connecticut

*Reading Consultant*
**Nanci R. Vargus**, *Ed.D.*
*Teacher in Residence*
*University of Indianapolis*
*Indianapolis, Indiana*

A young basketball player drives to the hoop.

Library of Congress Cataloging-in-Publication Data

Kennedy, Mike (Mike William), 1965-
   Basketball / by Mike Kennedy.
      p. cm. – (A True book)
   Includes bibliographical references and index.
   Summary: An introduction to basketball including history, rules, and a
list of some of the sport's outstanding players.
   ISBN 0-516-22335-6 (lib. bdg.)    0-516-29372-9 (pbk.)
1. Basketball—United States—Juvenile literature. [1. Basketball.] I. Title.
II. Series.

GV885.1.K47 2002
796.323—dc21

2001047200

CHILDREN'S PRESS, AND A TRUE BOOK®, and associated logos are
trademarks and or registered trademarks of Grolier Publishing Co., Inc.
SCHOLASTIC and associated logos are trademarks and or registered
trademarks of Scholastic Inc.

1 2 3 4 5 6 7 8 9 10 R 11 10 09 08 07 06 05 04 03 02

# Contents

Dr. James Naismith invented basketball in 1891.

# Hoops Story

In 1891, Dr. James Naismith was asked to create an indoor activity to occupy young men during Massachusetts's winter months. The next day, he nailed two peach baskets to the balcony in a YMCA gym. Then he told two teams of students to try to toss a soccer ball into the goals.

5

Soon, YMCAs everywhere hosted games of this new sport, now called basketball. It didn't look very much like the game you know. Today, of course, five players from each team take the court and try to shoot the ball into the **opponent's** basket. Tripping, holding, and pushing are not allowed.

Early versions of basketball, however, had more players and were extremely rough and low scoring. Around 1900, colleges began having basketball teams,

Early basketball games were very rough (above). From the beginning, girls (right) as well as boys enjoyed the sport.

and the modern game started to take shape. By the 1930s, basketball had become popular among young people nationwide.

7

The roots of **professional** basketball took hold during World War II. The National Basketball Association (NBA) formed in the years that followed. Basketball remained slow and low scoring until 1954, when the NBA introduced the 24-second shot clock. Now, whenever a team took possession (control) of the ball, they had to take a shot that hit the rim of the basket within 24 seconds, or the ball would go to the other team.

This quickened the pace of the game because teams were forced to shoot more often. In turn, the

For years, Michael Jordan was the NBA's main attraction.

spotlight was focused on players who could put the ball in the basket. The age of the superstar was born. To this day, though basketball is a team sport, star players are often the main attraction.

Young women playing basketball in the 1890s

# You Go, Girl!

**W**omen picked up basketball just weeks after Dr. Naismith invented the game. Over the years, they have put their own spin on the sport. Many people, in fact, prefer the teamwork of the women's game. That's a major reason why the Women's National Basketball Association (WNBA) is so popular.

Who is the greatest female player ever? Probably Cynthia Cooper, who won it all in college and the Olympics, and ended her career with four straight WNBA titles. Others of note are Nera White, Ann Donovan, Lucy Harris, Carol Blazejowski, Ann Meyers, Cheryl Miller, and Sheryl Swoopes. Many people feel, however, that Chamique Holdsclaw might become the best of them all.

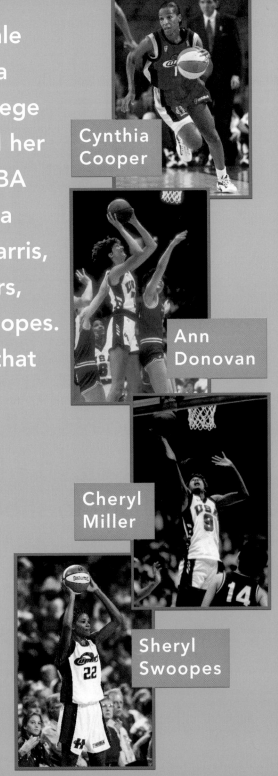

Cynthia Cooper

Ann Donovan

Cheryl Miller

Sheryl Swoopes

Chamique Holdsclaw rises for an easy basket.

# Old School, New Look

The first basketball was made in 1894. It was larger than today's ball, had laces like those on a football, and was hard to shoot and dribble. The modern ball **evolved** over the next 40 years, as the need grew for a smaller ball without laces that was easier to handle.

In the early days of basketball, the ball had laces.

Backboards did not come into use until 1896. They were necessary to stop spectators from interfering with shots. Fifty years later, colleges began using glass backboards to give a better view to fans behind the basket.

The modern net was introduced in 1913. Before that, players shot into a net without a hole in the bottom. After every basket, someone had to knock the ball free with a broom or long stick!

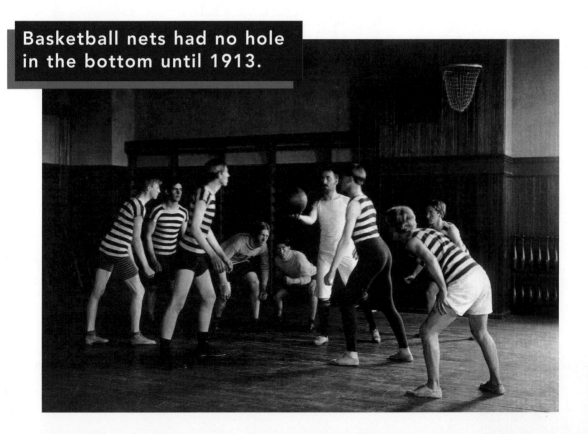

Basketball nets had no hole in the bottom until 1913.

Players in the early days wore tight shorts with heavy padding because the game was so rough. Sleeveless "tank-top" jerseys, however, have always been part of a basketball uniform.

Players also raced around in uncomfortable leather shoes with slick bottoms. Around 1900, sporting goods manufacturers began making special canvas basketball shoes with rubber bottoms to keep

Modern-day basketball sneakers

players from slipping. Those basic shoes remained in use until the 1970s, when today's more advanced sneakers started to appear.

# Let's Play!

The object in basketball is to outscore your opponent. There is more to the game, however, than shooting. Control of the ball switches constantly, which means every player is responsible for playing **offense** and **defense**. Referees make sure everyone plays by the rules.

Control of the ball switches constantly in basketball.

In a game, each team is assigned a hoop to defend. The teams switch hoops after halftime. These baskets are located at each end of the

An overhead view of a basketball court

court. The court is shaped like a rectangle and has lines running around the outside. When the ball bounces across one of these lines, it is out of bounds, and play stops.

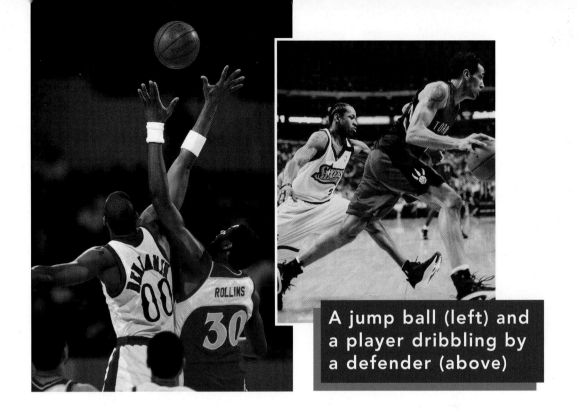

A jump ball (left) and a player dribbling by a defender (above)

Every game begins with a jump ball. The referee tosses the ball in the air and two players from opposite teams try to tip it to their teammates.

The squad that controls the ball goes on offense. Here the

A two-point shot (left) and a three-point shot (right)

goal is to get the easiest shot possible. As a general rule, the closer you are to the hoop, the better are your chances of scoring. All shots from the field are worth two points, unless taken from outside the three-point line. Then they count for three.

On defense, one's goal is to stop the other team from scoring. When playing defense, good players don't chase the ball all over the court. Instead, they pick an opponent to guard and stick close to that player. They must stay alert and keep their hands ready to deflect passes or steal the ball.

A player guarding an opponent with the ball (left) and a player going for a steal (right)

A shooter (in black jersey) getting fouled as he soars for a layup

When the referee blows the whistle, all action stops. For example, the "ref" can call a defensive player for a foul against an offensive player. This happens when a player gets too physical.

A player fouled while attempting a shot is awarded free throws from the foul line. Each successful free throw counts for one point.

A player attempting a free throw

Players can also commit offensive fouls. The most common is "charging." This occurs when a player knocks down a defender whose feet are set firmly on the floor.

Charging is a type of offensive foul.

A young player dribbling the ball (above) and a college player passing the ball (right)

How do you find open shots on offense? By dribbling the ball (bouncing it on the ground) and passing it around to your teammates. The more quickly you move the ball, the more likely it is that your team will create an open shot. Running with the ball without dribbling, however, is not allowed. Neither is dribbling with two hands, nor kicking the ball. You also can't bounce the ball, hold it, and then start dribbling it again. These are all known as violations. They mean that your team automatically loses possession of the ball.

Fouls have more serious **consequences** than violations. In the NBA, for instance, players are ejected from (made to leave) the game when they commit their sixth foul.

After a shot is taken, several things can happen. If the offensive team converts (makes) a basket, the other team gets the ball and moves down the court to try to score. If a shot misses, both teams go for the **rebound**.

Whichever team gains control
of the ball is on offense, while
the other plays defense. This
constant back-and-forth action
is one reason basketball is so
much fun.

# What's Your Position?

Each of the five positions in basketball has specific responsibilities. Some players specialize in scoring, while others shine on defense. The best are good at both.

Point guards run the show on offense. They must be able to handle the ball with

The point guard is his team's best ball handler (left). The off guard is counted on for scoring (right).

great skill and set up teammates for easy shots. They need quick feet to help them dribble around defenders and to the basket.

Off guards often are their team's best scorers. They need to shoot well far from the basket. Sometimes, they also have to make difficult shots when their teammates are not open.

Centers normally spend a lot of time near the hoop. Since they are usually the tallest players on the court, they try to set up close to the basket for easy lay-ins.

The center uses his size to muscle in for easy baskets.

The power forward is often the top rebounder on the floor (left). The small forward relies on speed to burst by the defense (right).

Power forwards also **jostle** for position close to the hoop. They rely on strong legs and shoulders to play defense and grab rebounds. Many of their points come after missed shots.

Small forwards are graceful athletes who play away from the basket and try to score close to the hoop. They handle the ball on occasion, and often convert baskets by running ahead of the defense without the ball and then receiving a pass for a **dunk**.

Each player on the floor guards an opponent, usually the one who plays the same position. Teams also are allowed to play "zone" defenses in which players are assigned a specific area on the court.

# Five on Five

## Here are 10 players who changed basketball:

Hank Luisetti

**Hank Luisetti, F, college: Stanford, 1934-38**
Everyone used the two-handed set shot until Hank introduced his running one-hander.

Bob Cousy

**Bob Cousy, G, college: Holy Cross, pro: 1950-63**
Cousy's fancy dribbling, no-look passing, and clutch scoring defined the role of the point guard.

Bill Russell

**Bill Russell, C, college: San Francisco, pro: 1956-69**
With 11 NBA championships, Russell showed that defense and rebounding were the keys to winning.

Elgin Baylor

**Elgin Baylor, F, college: Seattle, pro: 1958-72**
The graceful, high-flying Baylor took the game above the rim.

Wilt Chamberlain

**Wilt Chamberlain, C, college: Kansas, pro: 1959-73**
Wilt the Stilt, who once scored 100 points in an NBA game, was an offensive force like no other.

Oscar Robertson, G, college, Cincinnati, pro: 1960-73

The Big O averaged a **"triple-double"** during the 1961-62 NBA season.

Oscar Robertson

Magic Johnson, G, college: Michigan State, pro: 1979-91, 1996

Every game was "show time" for Magic, who proved that big men could play any position.

Magic Johnson

Larry Bird, F, college: Indiana State, pro: 1979-92

The Bird Man reminded us that there is much more to the game than the slam dunk.

Larry Bird

Michael Jordan, G, college: North Carolina, pro: 1984-93, 1994-98, 2001-present

Everybody wants to be like Mike, probably the greatest player who ever lived.

Michael Jordan

Kobe Bryant, G, pro: 1996-present

Bryant, who leaped from high school to the NBA, is basketball's poster boy for the new millennium.

Kobe Bryant

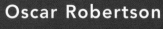

# Pros and Colleges

Are there differences between professional and college basketball? Sure. Professional games are divided into four 12-minute quarters, while college games are divided into two 20-minute halves. Also, the three-point line in the pros is farther out.

What is the biggest difference? College basketball coaches develop "systems" that stress teamwork. The NBA, by contrast, relies on the star power of its best players.

In college basketball, the coach develops and teaches his own system.

College basketball had a head start on the NBA of nearly 50 years. During that time, universities realized the importance of a good coach. Every year, a class of seniors graduated and a new group of players joined the team. It was the coach's job to mold this collection of players into his system.

To compete with the colleges, the NBA had to find a way to thrill fans. The league promoted the individual talents of its most exciting players, whose careers often lasted for 10 years or more.

For example, center George Mikan led the Minneapolis Lakers to the

NBA championship in four of the league's first five seasons. Soon after, forward Bob Pettit became a scoring sensation for the St. Louis Hawks. Sweet-shooting guard Jerry West was the most dangerous player in the 1960s. During the following decades, Julius Erving, Pete Maravich, David Thompson, and Dominique Wilkins were among those who delighted fans. Shaquille O'Neal and Vince Carter have taken the torch from them.

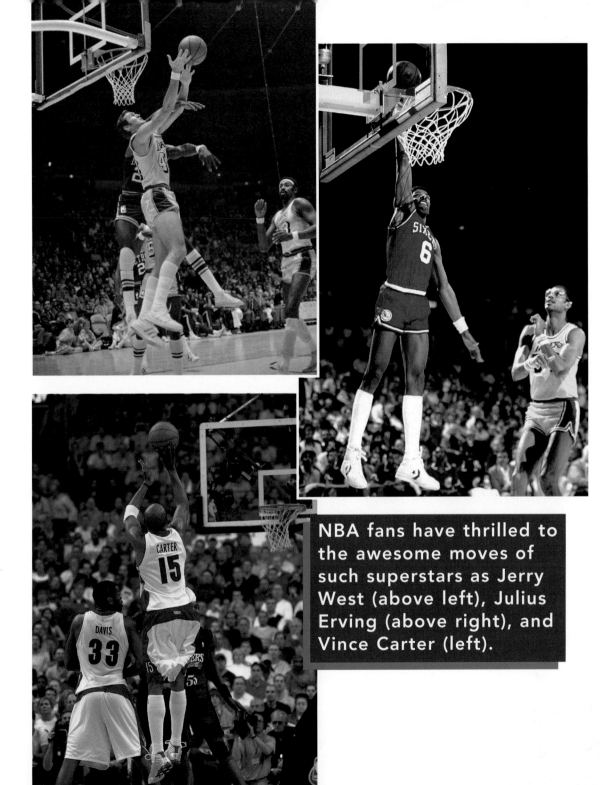

NBA fans have thrilled to the awesome moves of such superstars as Jerry West (above left), Julius Erving (above right), and Vince Carter (left).

# To Find Out More

Here are some additional resources to help you learn more about basketball:

 **Books**

Kramer, S.A. **Basketball's Greatest Players.** Random House, 1997.

Mullin, Chris and Coleman, Brian. **The Young Basketball Player.** DK Publishing, 1995.

Rutledge, Rachel. **The Best of the Best in Basketball**. The Millbrook Press, 1998.

Stewart, Mark. **Basketball: A History of Hoops.** Franklin Watts, 1998.

## Organizations and Online Sites

**Naismith Memorial Basketball Hall of Fame**
*http://www.hoophall.com*

Provides information on the legends of basketball honored there.

**National Basketball Association**
*http://www.nba.com*

Offers the latest scores, standings, and news on every player in the NBA.

**USA Basketball**
*http://www.usabasketball.com*

Provides information on every U.S. national basketball team, both men's and women's.

**Women's National Basketball Association**
*http://www.wnba.com*

Offers the latest scores, standings, and news on every player in the WNBA.

*http://www.basketball.com*

Comprehensive site that offers information on all levels of basketball, from youth leagues and high school to the pros.

# Important Words

**defense** in basketball, trying to keep the opposing team from scoring

**dunk** to slam a basketball into the basket from above the rim

**evolved** gradually changed

**jostle** to push roughly

**offense** in basketball, trying to score points

**opponent** person or team one is playing against

**possession** in basketball, having control of the ball

**rebound** act of gaining possession of the basketball after another player shoots and misses

**system** in basketball, the way a coach teaches the game and builds his team

**triple-double** when a player earns double digits in points, rebounds, and assists all in one game

# Index

# Meet the Author

Mike Kennedy is a freelance sportswriter whose work has ranged from Super Bowl coverage to historical research and analysis. He has profiled athletes in virtually every sport, including Peyton Manning, Bernie Williams, and Allen Iverson. He is a graduate of Franklin & Marshall College in Lancaster, Pennsylvania.

Mike has contributed his expertise to other books for young people, including *Auto Racing: A History of Fast Cars and Fearless Drivers.* He has authored four sports True Books, including *Football* and *Baseball.*

Photographs © 2002: AllSport USA/Getty Images: 43 top right (Andrew D. Bernstein/NBA Photos), 11 top center right (Alvin Chung), 37 bottom left (Jonathan Daniel/NBA Photos), 26 (Barry Gossage/NBA Photos), 11 bottom left (Otto Greule/WNBA Photos), 24, 33, 43 bottom left (M. David Leeds/NBA Photos), 37 center right (NBA Photos), 20, 22 left (Doug Pensinger), 22 right (Doug Pensinger/NBA Photos), 40 (Ezra Shaw); AP/Wide World Photos: 36 top left (Stanford University), 36 bottom left; Archive Photos/Getty Images: 36 center left (Larry C. Morris/New York Times Co); Brian Spurlock: 37 bottom right; Brown Brothers: 10, 13, 14; Corbis Images: 21 right (Ron J. Berard/Duomo), 4, 7 left, 36 top right, 36 bottom right, 37 top right, 43 top left (Bettmann), 34 right (Jim Bourg/Reuters NewMedia Inc.), 39 (Gary Brady/Reuters NewMedia Inc.), 2, 32 right (Greg Flume/Duomo), 11 bottom center right (Wally McNamee), 7 right (Minnesota Historical Society), 34 left (Jeff Mitchell/Reuters NewMedia Inc.), 9, 27 right (Sue Ogrocki/Reuters NewMedia Inc.), 32 left (Robert Padgett/Reuters NewMedia Inc.), 1, 27 left (William Sallaz/Duomo), 23 left (Ray Stubblebine/Reuters NewMedia Inc.), 23 right (Jason Wise/Duomo), 15; Icon Sports Media: 21 left (John McDonough), 17 (John McDonough/SI), 11 bottom right; SportsChrome USA: 25 (Brian Drake), 37 top left (David L. Johnson), 11 top right (Michael Zito); The Image Works/Steve Warmowski/Jacksonville Journal-Courier: cover, 19, 30.